Graham Greene

A Checklist of Criticism

Graham Greene

A Checklist of Criticism

by J. Don Vann
North Texas State University

The Kent State University Press

The Serif Series:
Bibliographies and Checklists, Number 14

William White, General Editor
Wayne State University

ISBN 0-87338-101-7
Library of Congress Catalog Card Number 70-113763
Manufactured in the United States of America
at the press of The Oberlin Printing Company.
Designed by Merald E. Wrolstad

First Edition

Foreword

This checklist is designed to serve as a tool for the researcher by providing a compilation of criticism about Graham Greene. Adequate bibliographies of Greene's writings are available elsewhere.

Of the bibliographies listed in the first section, four of them are worth comment: that by Mr. Birmingham is an essay which selects what the compiler thought the best of Greene criticism up to 1952; Miss Hargreaves's is a 1957 bibliography of work by Greene; Mr. Beebe's is a selected checklist of about one hundred books and articles on Greene, also to 1957; and the Brennan selected checklist includes about three hundred and fifty books and articles. My own covers, hopefully, omissions from the previous lists, almost doubles the number of entries in Brennan, and brings Greene scholarship from 1963 up to date.

I must acknowledge my indebtedness to those bibliographers cited in the section on bibliographies, to the Committee on Faculty Research of North Texas State University for providing released time from teaching duties, and to my research assistant, Betty Burke, for her diligence.

J. Don Vann

Contents

A. Bibliographies

Beebe, Maurice. "Criticism of Graham Greene: A Selected Checklist with an Index to Studies of Separate Works," *Modern Fiction Studies*, III (Autumn 1957), 281–288.

Birmingham, William. "Graham Greene Criticism: A Bibliographical Study," *Thought*, XXVII (Spring 1952), 72–100.

Brennan, Neil. "Bibliography," in Robert O. Evans, ed., *Graham Greene*. Lexington: University of Kentucky Press, 1963, pp. 245–276.

Hargreaves, Phylis. "Graham Greene: A Selected Bibliography," *Modern Fiction Studies*, III (Autumn 1957), 269–280.

———. "Graham Greene: A Selective Bibliography," *Bulletin of Bibliography*, XXII (January 1954), 45–48.

Remords, G. "Graham Greene: Notes Biographiques et Bibliographiques," *Bulletin de la Faculté des Lettres de Strasbourg*, XXIX (May–June 1951), 393–399.

Wyndham, Francis. *Graham Greene.* (*Writers and Their Work,* No. 67.) London: Longmans, 1955.

Unsigned. "A Bibliography of Graham Greene," *Marginalia,* II (April 1951), 16–19.

B. Books About Greene

Allott, Kenneth, and Miriam Farris. *The Art of Graham Greene.* London: Hamish Hamilton, 1951; New York: Russell & Russell, 1963.

REVIEWS:

Allen, Walter. *New Statesman and Nation,* XLI (June 16, 1951), 685.

Mayberry, George. *New York Times,* October 28, 1951, p. 5.

Unsigned. *Manchester Guardian,* LXIV (June 8, 1951), 4.

———. *Times Literary Supplement* (London), June 8, 1951, p. 358.

Atkins, John. *Graham Greene: A Biographical and Literary Study.* London: J. Calder, 1957 (Revised in 1966); New York: Roy Publishers, 1958.

REVIEWS:

Blakeston, O. *Books and Bookmen,* XII (April 1967), 44.

Burgess, Anthony. *Manchester Guardian,* XCV (November 17, 1966), 11.

Finn, James. *Commonweal,* LXIX (December 5, 1958), 268.

Pritchett, V. S. *New Statesman,* LV (January 4, 1958), 4.

Raven, Simon. *Spectator*, CXCVIII (November 22, 1957), 704.

Shrapnel, Norman. *Manchester Guardian*, November 29, 1957, p. 13.

Unsigned. *Choice*, IV (July-August 1967), 529.

Dellevaux, Raymond. *Graham Greene et "Le Fond du Problème."* Brussels: Editions "La Lecture au Foyer," 1951.

DeVitis, A. A. *Graham Greene*. New York: Twayne Publishers, 1964.

REVIEWS:

Lodge, D. *Modern Language Review*, LX (October 1965), 607.

Evans, R. O., ed. *Graham Greene: Some Critical Considerations*. Lexington: University of Kentucky Press, 1963.

REVIEWS:

McDonnell, T. P. *Commonweal*, LXXIX (March 13, 1964), 727–729.

Woodbridge, H. C. *American Book Collector*, XIV (March 1964), 5.

Fournier, Gaston, S. J. *Le Tourment de Dieu Chez les Amants de Graham Greene*. Toulouse: Imprimerie Parisienne, 1953.

———. *Scobie, ou l'homme victime de sa pitié: "Le Fond du Problème" de Graham Greene*. Toulouse: Imprimerie Parisienne, 1953.

Ibáñez Langlois, José Miguel. *El Mundo Pecador de Graham Greene*. Santiago de Chile: Zig-Zag, 1967.

Kohn, Lynette. *Graham Greene: The Major Novels.* Palo Alto: Stanford Honors Essays in Humanities, no. IV, 1961.

Kunkel, F. L. *The Labyrinthine Ways of Graham Greene.* New York: Sheed and Ward, 1959.

REVIEWS:

Boyle, R. R. *America,* CV (January 14, 1961), 478–479.

Callahan, Edward F. *Thought,* XXVI (Winter 1961), 618–620.

Clancy, Joseph P. *Catholic World,* CXCII (January 1961), 248–249.

Deasy, P. *Commonweal,* LXXIII (December 9, 1960), 295–297.

Hicks, Granville. *Saturday Review,* XLIII (December 17, 1960), 16.

Schlueter, Paul. *Christian Century,* LXXVIII (February 22, 1961), 243–244.

Wills, G. *National Review,* X (January 28, 1961), 58.

Lodge, David. *Graham Greene.* New York: Columbia University Press, 1966.

REVIEWS:

Unsigned. *Choice,* III (November 1966), 771.

Madaule, Jacques. *Graham Greene.* Paris: Editions du Temps Présent, 1949.

Matthews, Ronald. *Mon Ami Graham Greene.* Paris: Desclée de Brouwer, 1957.

Mesnet, Marie-Beatrice. *Graham Greene and the Heart of the Matter.* London: Cresset Press, 1954.

REVIEWS:

Unsigned. *Times Literary Supplement* [London], July 9, 1954, p. 438.

Pange, Victor de. *Graham Greene*. Paris: Editions Universitaires, 1953.

Pryce-Jones, David. *Graham Greene*. Edinburgh: Oliver and Boyd, 1963.

Rischik, Josef. *Graham Greene und sein Werk*. Bern: A. Francke, 1951.

Rostenne, Paul. *Graham Greene: Témoin des Temps Tragiques*. Paris: Juillard, 1949.

Stratford, Philip. *Faith and Fiction: Creative Process in Greene and Mauriac*. Notre Dame: University of Notre Dame Press, 1964.

REVIEWS:

Cottrell, B. W. *Christian Century*, LXXXI (November 11, 1964), 1406.

DeVitis, A. A. *Renascence*, XIII (Summer 1961), 216–217.

Dooley, D. J. *Dalhousie Review*, XLV (Spring 1965), 100–103.

Falconer, Graham. *University of Toronto Quarterly*, XXXIV (July 1965), 393–395.

Gaines, E. J. *Library Journal*, LXXXIX (September 15, 1964), 3316.

Mason, H. T. *Notes and Queries*, CCXI (March 1966), 111–112.

Smith, A. J. M. *Queen's Quarterly*, LXXII (Summer 1965), 419.

West, Paul. *Canadian Forum*, XLIV (February 1965), 263.

Sturzl, Erwin. *Von Satan zu Gott: Religiöse Probleme bei Graham Greene*. Vienna: Graph. Lerh. und Versuchs-Anstalt, 1954.

Turnell, Martin. *Graham Greene: A Critical Essay*. Grand Rapids: Eerdmans, 1967.

C. Chapters About Greene and References to Greene in Books

Alder, Jacob H. "Graham Greene's Plays: Technique Versus Value." In *Graham Greene: Some Critical Considerations*, edited by Robert O. Evans. Lexington: University of Kentucky Press, 1963, pp. 219–230.

Albérès, R.-M. "Graham Greene et la responsabilité." *Les Hommes Traques*. Paris: La Nouvelle Editions, 1953, pp. 157–185.

Allen, Walter. "Graham Greene." In *Writers of Today*, edited by Denys Val Baker. London: Sidgwick, 1946, pp. 15–28.

———. "Seven Novels Discussed." *Reading a Novel*. London: Phoenix Books, 1956, pp. 37–42.

Allott, Miriam. "The Moral Situation in *The Quiet American*." In *Graham Greene: Some Critical Considerations*, edited by Robert O. Evans. Lexington: University of Kentucky Press, 1963, pp. 188–206.

Atkins, John. "Altogether Amen: A Reconsideration of *The Power and the Glory*." In *Graham Greene: Some Critical Considerations*, edited by Robert O. Evans. Lexington: University of Kentucky Press, 1963, pp. 181–187.

———. "The Curse of the Film." In *Graham Greene: Some Critical Considerations*, edited by Robert O. Evans. Lexington: University of Kentucky Press, 1963, pp. 207–218.

Beaton, Cecil W. H., and Kenneth Tynan. *Persona Grata.* New York: Putnam, 1954, pp. 53–56.

Bernoville, Gáetan. "Introduction." In *Le Catholicisme dans l'oeuvre de François Mauriac*, edited by Robert J. North. Paris: Editions du Conquistador, 1950.

Browne, E. M. "Contemporary Drama in the Catholic Tradition." In *Christian Faith and the Contemporary Arts*, edited by F. Eversole. Nashville: Abingdon, 1962, pp. 132–141.

Buckler, William E., and Arnold B. Sklare. *Stories from Six Authors.* New York: McGraw-Hill, 1960.

Calder-Marshall, Arthur. "Graham Greene." In *Living Writers: Being Critical Studies Broadcast in the B.B.C. Third Programme*, edited by Gilbert Phelps. London: Sylvan Press, 1947, pp. 39–47.

Chaigne, Louis. "Graham Greene." *Vies et Oeuvres d'Ecrivains.* Paris: F. Lanore, 1952, pp. 195–237.

Church, Richard. "Graham Greene." *British Authors.* Longmans, 1948, pp. 137–140.

Connolly, Francis. *The Types of Literature.* New York: Harcourt, Brace, 1955, pp. 706–707.

Consolo, Dominick P. "Graham Greene: Style and Stylistics in Five Novels." In *Graham Greene: Some Critical Considerations*, edited by Robert O. Evans. Lexington: University of Kentucky Press, 1963, pp. 61–95.

Davis, H. "The Confessional and the Altar." *A Mirror of the Ministry in Modern Novels*. New York: Oxford, 1959, pp. 81–110.

DeVitis, A. A. "The Catholic as Novelist: Graham Greene and François Mauriac." In *Graham Greene: Some Critical Considerations*, edited by Robert O. Evans. Lexington: University of Kentucky Press, 1963, pp. 112–126.

Engel, Claire Elaine. "Graham Greene." *Esquisses Anglaises* (Paris, Editions "Je Sera," 1949), pp. 57–98.

Evans, Robert O. "The Satanist Fallacy of *Brighton Rock*." In *Graham Greene: Some Critical Considerations*, edited by Robert O. Evans. Lexington: University of Kentucky Press, 1963, pp. 151–168.

Frederiksen, Emil. "Graham Greene." In *Fremmede digtere i det 20. århundrede*, edited by Sven M. Kristensen. Copenhagen: G.E.C. Grad., 1968, III, pp. 199–213.

Gable, Sister Mariella. *This Is Catholic Fiction*. New York: Sheed and Ward, 1948, passim.

Gardiner, H. C. "Mr. Greene Does It Again." In *In All Conscience*. New York: Hanover House, 1959, pp. 96–98.

———. "Second Thoughts on Greene's Latest." In *In All Conscience*. New York: Hanover House, 1959, pp. 98–102.

Gassner, J. "Points of Return: Religion and Graham Greene's *The Potting Shed*." In *Theatre at the Crossroads*. New York: Holt, Rinehart & Winston, 1960, pp. 155–157.

Graff, Hilda. "Graham Greene." *Modern Gloom and Christian Hope*. (Chicago: Regnery, 1959), pp. 84–97.

Gregor, Ian, and Brian Nicholas. "Grace and Morality: 'Thérèse Desqueyroux.'" *The Moral and the Story*. London: Faber and Faber, 1962, pp. 185–216.

Guitton, Jean. "Ya-t-il encore une nature humaine?" *L'Humanisme et la Grâce*. Paris: Edition de Flore, 1950, pp. 125–142.

Haber, Herbert R. "The End of the Catholic Cycle: The Writer Versus the Saint." In *Graham Greene: Some Critical Considerations*, edited by Robert O. Evans. Lexington: University of Kentucky Press, 1963, pp. 127–150.

Hall, James. "Efficient Saints and Civilians: Graham Greene." *The Lunatic Giant in the Drawing Room*: *The British and American Novel Since 1930*. Bloomington: Indiana University Press, 1968, pp. 111–123.

Havighurst, Walter. "Study of 'Across the Bridge.'" *Instructor's Manual: Masters of the Modern Short Story*. New York: Harcourt, Brace, 1955, pp. 27–28.

Heilman, Robert B. *Modern Short Stories: A Critical Anthology*. New York: Harcourt, Brace, 1950, pp. 264–266.

Hesla, David H. "Theological Ambiguity in the 'Catholic Novels.'" In *Graham Greene: Some Critical Considerations*, edited by Robert O. Evans. Lexington: University of Kentucky Press, 1963, pp. 96–111.

Hoehn, Matthew, ed. "Graham Greene." *Catholic Authors*. St. Mary's Abbey, 1948, pp. 289–290.

Jonsson, Thorsten Georg. "Ett Portrait av Scobie." *Tva Essayer om Graham Greene. Stockholm*: *Norstedts*, 1950, pp. 1–8.

Joselyn, Sister M., O.S.B. "Graham Greene's Novels: The Conscience in the World." In *Literature and Society*, edited by B. Slote. Lincoln: University of Nebraska Press, 1964, pp. 153–172.

Karl, F. R. "Graham Greene's Demoniacal Heroes." In *The Contemporary English Novel*. New York: Farrar, Straus, & Company, 1962, pp. 85–106.

Kazin, Alfred. "Graham Greene and the Age of Absurdity." In *Contemporaries*. Boston: Little, Brown & Company, 1962, pp. 158–161.

Kermode, J. F. "Mr. Greene's Eggs and Crosses." In *Puzzles and Epiphanies*. New York: Chilmark Press, 1962, pp. 176–187.

Kerr, Walter. "*The Complaisant Lover*" In *The Theater in Spite of Itself*. New York: Simon & Schuster, 1963, pp. 157–160.

———. "Playwrights." In *Pieces at Eight*. New York: Simon & Schuster, 1957, pp. 117–149.

Kettle, Arnold. *An Introduction to the English Novel*. London: Hutchinson, 1953, II, pp. 170–177.

Knaak Peuser, Angélica. "La Novela de Graham Greene." *El E spiritu y la Carne en las Grandes Creaciones Literarias*. Bueno Aires, Ediciones Peuser, 1952, pp. 161–179.

Kunkel, Francis L. "The Theme of Sin and Grace in Graham Greene." In *Graham Greene: Some Critical Considerations*, edited by Robert O. Evans. Lexington: University of Kentucky Press, 1963, pp. 49–60.

Kuntz, Stanley J[assdon], ed. "Graham Greene." *Twentieth Century Authors*, First Supplement. New York: Wilson, 1942, pp. 572–573.

Laitinen, Kai. "The Heart of the Novel: The Turning Point in *The Heart of the Matter*." In *Graham Greene: Some Critical Considerations*, edited by Robert O. Evans. Lexington: University of Kentucky Press, 1963, pp. 169–180.

Levi, Albert William. *Literature, Philosophy and the Imagination*. Bloomington: Indiana University Press, 1962, *passim*.

Lewis, R. W. B. "Graham Greene: The Religious Affair." In *The Picaresque Saint: Representative Figures in Contemporary Fiction*. Philadelphia and New York: Lippincott, 1959, pp. 220–274.

Lindegren, Erik. "Graham Greene." *Tva Essayer om Graham Greene*. Stockholm: Norstedts, 1950, pp. 9–16.

Lumley, F. "Britain." In *New Trends in 20th Century Drama*, New York: Oxford, 1967, pp. 255–316.

Lynskey, Winifred. *Reading Modern Fiction: 30 Stories with Study Aids*. New York: Scribners, 1952, pp. 245–246.

Mauriac, Francois. "Graham Greene." In *Great Men*. London: Rockliff, 1952, pp. 117–121.

Moeller, Charles. "Graham Green ou le martyre de l'espérance." *Littérature Du XXe Siecle et Christianisme: I: Silence De Dieu*. Tournai, Belgium: Casterman, 1953, pp. 259–301.

Mueller, W. R. "Theme of Love: Graham Greene's *The Heart of the Matter*." In *Prophetic Voice in Modern Fiction*. New York: Association Press, 1959, pp. 136–157.

Newby, P. H. "Character and Situation: Graham Greene, Joyce Cary and L. P. Hartley." *The Novel, 1945–1950*. London: Longmans, 1951, pp. 33–36.

O'Donnell, Donat. "Graham Greene: The Anatomy of Pity." *Maria Cross: Imaginative Patterns in a Group of Modern Catholic Writers*. New York: Oxford University Press, 1952, pp. 61–91.

O'Faoláin, Sean. "Graham Greene." In *Vanishing Hero*. Boston: Little, Brown & Co., 1957, pp. 45–72.

———. "Graham Greene: I Suffer; Therefore, I Am." *The Vanishing Hero: Studies in Novelists of the Twenties*. London: Eyre and Spottiswoode, 1956, pp. 73–97.

Prescott, Orville. "Comrades of the Coterie: Henry Green, Compton-Burnett, Bowen, Graham Greene." In *In My Opinion*. Indianapolis: Bobbs-Merrill, 1952, pp. 92–109.

Reed, Henry. *The Novel since 1939*. London: Longmans, 1947, pp. 15–18.

Sale, William M., Jr., James Hall and Martin Steinmann, Jr. *Critical Discussions for Teachers Using "Short Stories: Tradition and Direction*." Norfolk, Connecticut: New Directions, 1949, pp. 62–64.

Schorer, Mark. *The Story: A Critical Anthology*. New York: Prentice-Hall, 1950, pp. 183–185.

Scott, Carolyn D. "The Witch at the Corner: Notes on Graham Greene's Mythology." In *Graham Greene: Some Critical Considerations*, edited by Robert O. Evans. Lexington: University of Kentucky Press, 1963, pp. 231–244.

Scott, Nathan A., Jr. "Graham Greene: Christian Tragedian." In *Graham Greene: Some Critical Considerations*, edited by Robert O. Evans. Lexington: University of Kentucky Press, 1963, pp. 25–48.

Stewart, Douglas. "Catholicism." In *The Ark of God*. London: Carey Kingsgate Press Ltd., 1961, pp. 71–98.

Tynan, Kenneth. "*The Living Room*, by Graham Greene, at Wyndam's." In *Curtains*. New York: Atheneum, 1961, pp. 47–49.

———. "*The Potting Shed*, by Graham Greene, at the Globe." In *Curtains*. New York: Atheneum, 1961, pp. 207–209.

Webster, Harvey Curtis. "The World of Graham Greene." In *Graham Greene: Some Critical Considerations*, edited by Robert O. Evans. Lexington: University of Kentucky Press, 1963, pp. 1–24.

West, Anthony. "Graham Greene." In *Principles and Persuasions*. New York: Harcourt, Brace, 1957, pp. 195–200.

West, Paul. "Graham Greene." In *The Wine of Absurdity*. University Park: Pennsylvania State University Press, 1966, pp. 174–185.

Wilshere, A. D. "Conflict and Conciliation in Graham Greene." In *Essays and Studies, 1966*, edited by R. M. Wilson. New York: Humanities Press, 1966, pp. 122–137.

Woodcock, George. "Graham Greene." In *The Writer and Politics*. London: Porcupine Press, 1948, pp. 125–153.

Zabel, M. D. "Graham Greene: The Best and the Worst." In *Craft and Character in Modern Fiction*. New York: Viking, 1957, pp. 276–296. Slightly different versions were published in *Critiques and Essays on Modern Fiction, 1920–1951*, edited by J. W. Albridge, New York: Ronald Press, 1952, pp. 518–525; and in *Forms of Modern Fiction*, edited by William Van O'Conner, Minneapolis: University of Minnesota Press, 1948, pp. 287–293.

D. Articles About Greene

Abirached, R. "Le Paria de Graham Greene," *Etudes*, no. 11 (November 1963), pp. 241–244.

Aguirre De Carcer, Nuno. "La novela en la Inglaterra actual: II. Graham Greene," *Arbor*, XIV (September–October 1949), 99–113.

Allen, W. Gore. "Another View of Graham Greene," *Catholic World*, CLXIX (April 1949), 69–70.

———. "Evelyn Waugh and Graham Greene," *Irish Monthly*, LXXVII (January 1949), 16–22.

———. "The World of Graham Greene," *Irish Ecclesiastical Record*, LXXI (January 1949), 42–49.

Allen, Walter. "Awareness of Evil: Graham Greene," *Nation*, CLXXXII (April 21, 1957), 344–346.

Alloway, Lawrence. "Symbolism in *The Third Man*," *World Review*, new series no. 13 (March 1950), pp. 57–60.

Anisimov, I. "Graham Greene's Novels," *Inostrannaya Literatura*, no. 10 (October 1964), pp. 221–226.

Arnesen, Axel. "Graham Greenes idéverden," *Samtiden*, LXXII (November 1963), 636–644.

Auden, W. H. "The Heresy of Our Time," *Renascence*, I (Spring 1949), 23–24. Also printed in *The Wind and the Rain*, VI (Summer 1949), 53–54.

Barlow, G. "L'Art de Graham Greene," *Esprit*, XXVII (March 1959), 517–525.

Barnes, Robert J. "Two Modes of Fiction: Hemingway and Greene," *Renascence*, XIV (Summer 1962), 193–198.

Barra, Giovanni. "La Conversione di Graham Greene," *Vita e Pensiero*, XXXVI (July 1953), 310–315.

Barratt, Harold. "Adultery as Betrayal in Graham Greene," *Dalhousie Review*, XLV (1965), 324–332.

Battock, Marjorie. "The Novels of Graham Greene," *The Norseman*, XIII (January–February 1955), 45–52.

Beary, Thomas John. "Religion and the Modern Novel," *Catholic World*, CLXVI (December 1947), 203–211.

Bechner, Hubert. "Der Stille Amerikaner," *Stimmen der Zeit*, CLX (April 1957), 68–72.

———. "Priestegestalten in der Romanliteratur der Gegenwart," *Stimmen der Zeit*, CLIII (1953), 345–355.

Bedard, Bernard John. "The Thriller Pattern in the Major Novels of Graham Greene," *Dissertation Abstracts*, XX (1959), 1779–1780.

Beirnaert, Louis. "Die menschliche Armseligkeit und die Gnade: Zu Graham Greenes Gestalten," *Universitas*, V (November 1950), 395–397.

———. "Does Sanctification Depend on Psychic Structure?" *Cross Currents*, no. 2 (Winter 1951), pp. 39–43.

Beltzikoff, Boris. "Kaj Munk och Graham Greene: En studie i Kristen Kriminologi," *Ord och Bild*, LXVI (1957), 249–258, 331–336.

Bentley, P. "Is the British Novel Dead?" *Saturday Review of Literature*, XIX (January 28, 1939), 4.

Blanchet, André. "Un nouveau 'Type' de Prêtre dans le roman contemporain," *Etudes*, no. 279 (February 1954), pp. 145–164 and no. 280 (March 1954), pp. 303–310.

Boardman, Gwenn Rosina. "Graham Greene: The Aesthetics of Exploration," *Dissertation Abstracts*, XXIV (1963), 2474.

———. "Greene's 'Under the Garden': Aesthetic Explorations," *Renascence*, XVII (1965), 180–190, 194.

Bouscaren, Anthony T. "France and Graham Greene versus America and Diem," *Catholic World*, CLXXXI (September 1955), 414–417.

Bowen, Elizabeth. "Story, Theme, and Situation," *Listener*, LVI (October 25, 1956), 651–652.

Boyle, Alexander. "Graham Greene," *Irish Monthly*, LXXVII (November 1949), 319–325.

———. "The Symbolism of Graham Greene," *Irish Monthly*, LXXX (1952), 98–102.

Boyle, Raymond M. "Man of Controversy," *Grail*, XXXV (July 1952), 1–7.

Brady, Charles A. "Contemporary Catholic Authors: Graham Greene, Novelist of Good and Evil." *Catholic Library World*, XVI (December 1944), 67–74, 89.

———. "Melodramatic Cousin in R. L. S.," *America*, LXIV (January 25, 1941), 439–440.

Brandstrup, Ole. "Til Helvede med succesen," *Perspektiv* (*Det danske magasin*), VIII (1961), 47–50.

Braybrooke, Neville. "End to Anguish?" *Commonweal*, LXIII (January 20, 1956), 406–407.

———. "Graham Greene," *Envoy*, III (September 1950), 10–23.

———. "Graham Greene: A Pioneer Novelist," *College English*, XII (October 1950), 1–9 .

———. "Graham Greene and the Double Man: An Approach to *The End of the Affair*," *Dublin Review*, CCXXVI (First Quarter 1952), 61–73.

———. "Graham Greene as Critic," *Commonweal*, LIV (July 6, 1951), 312–314.

Brennan, Neil. "Coney Island Rock," *Accent*, XVI (Spring 1956), 140–142.

Brion, Marcel. "Les romans de Graham Greene," *Revue des Deux Mondes*, no. 6 (March 15, 1950), pp. 367–375.

Brissaud, André. "C'est un champ de bataille/ C'est un homme traqué/ C'est l'univers de Graham Greene," *Arts*, no. 434 (October 22, 1953), p. 5.

Browne, E. M. "Graham Greene: Theatre's Gain," *Theatre Arts*, XLV (November 1961), 20–24.

Bryden, Ronald. "Graham Greene, Alas," *Spectator*, CCIX (September 28, 1962), 441–442.

Calder-Marshall, Arthur. "The Works of Graham Greene," *Horizon*, I (May 1940), 367–375.

Camilucci, Marcello. "Saggi cattolici di Graham Greene," *Studium*, LIV (December 1958), 823–830.

Cassidy, John. "America and Innocence: Henry James and Graham Greene," *Blackfrairs*, XXXVIII (June 1957), 261–267.

Castelli, Ferdinando. "Graham Greene, un romanziere che afascina e sconcerta," *Letture*, XVII (1962), 563–580.

Cayrol, Jean. "Autour de l'oeuvre de Graham Greene," *Revue de la Pensée Française*, X (April 1951), 68–72.

Chaigne, Louis. "Graham Greene," *Vies et Oeuvres d'écrivains*, III (1950), 193–237.

Chapman, Raymond. "The Vision of Graham Greene," *Forms of Extremity*, no. 19 (1965), pp. 77–94.

Chavardes, Maurice. "Graham Greene, ou La Nudité de Dieu," *Vie Intellectuelle*, no. 7 (July 1950), pp. 113–117.

Choisy, Maryse. "Psychoanalysis and Catholicism," *Cross Currents*, no. 3 (1951), pp. 75–90.

Clancy, W. "The Moral Burden of Mr. Greene's Parable," *Commonweal*, LXIII (March 16, 1956), 622.

Clurman, Robert. "The Quiet Englishman," *New York Times Book Review*, (August 26, 1956), p. 8.

Codey, Regina. "Notes on Graham Greene's Dramatic Technique." *Approach*, XVII (1955), 23–27.

Connolly, Francis X. "The Heart of the Matter." *Newsletter: Catholic Book Club*, XL (Midsummer 1948), 1–2.

———. "Inside Modern Man: The Spiritual Adventures of Graham Greene," *Renascence*, I (Spring 1949), 16–23.

Consolo, Dominick P. "Music as Motif: The Unity of *Brighton Rock*," *Renascence*, XV (Fall 1962), 12–20.

———. "The Technique of Graham Greene: A Stylistic Analysis of Five Novels," *Dissertation Abstracts*, XX (1959), 297.

Cooney, T. E. "Author as Traveler," *Saturday Review*, XXXIX (March 10, 1956), 12.

Cosman, Max. "Disquieted Graham Greene," *Colorado Quarterly*, VI (Winter 1958), 319–325.

———. "An Early Chapter in Graham Greene," *Arizona Quarterly*, XI (Summer 1955), 143–147.

Costello, Donald P. "Graham Greene and the Catholic Press," *Renascence*, XII (Autumn 1950), 3–28.

———. "The Latest in Greene Criticism," *Renascence*, XII (Autumn 1959), 38–40.

Cottrell, Beekman W. "Second Time Charm: The Theatre of Graham Greene," *Modern Fiction Studies*, III (Autumn 1957), 249–255.

Crubellier, Maurice. "Graham Greene: La Tragédie de la Pitié," *Vie Intellectuelle*, no. 12 (December 1951), pp. 57–58.

Currie, John Sheldon. "Supernaturalism in Graham Greene: A Comparison of Orthodox Catholicism with the Religious Vision in the Major Novels," *Dissertation Abstracts*, XXVIII (1968), 3176A–3177A.

Curtis, Jean-Louis. "Impressions de Londres," *La Table Ronde*, no. 1 (1948), pp. 155–158.

Davidson, Richard Allan. "Graham Greene and L. P. Hartley: 'The Basement Room' and *The Go-Between*," *Notes and Queries*, XIII (March 1966), 101–102.

Decap, Roger. "La tradition puritaine dans la littérature anglaise: John Bunyan et Graham Greene," *Caliban*, n.s. I (1965), 129–145.

Déchet, Ferruccio. "Suggestioni e limili della tematica di Graham Greene," *Giornalo di Metafisica*, XIX (1964), 75–89.

De Hegedus, Adam. "Graham Greene and the Modern Novel," *Tomorrow*, VIII (October 1948), 54–56.

———. "Graham Greene: The Man and His Work," *World Review*, (August 1948), pp. 57–61.

De La Bedoyere, Michael. "From My Window in Fleet Street," *Catholic World*, CXXIV (October 1951), 56–61.

Delpech, Jeanine. "Graham Greene à Paris," *Nouvelles Litéraires*, (December 19, 1946), pp. 1–2.

Delteil, F. "Romanciers catholiques anglais: II. Graham Greene," *Livres et Lectures*, no. 17 (1948), pp. 433–435.

De Vitis, A. A. "Allegory in *Brighton Rock*," *Modern Fiction Studies*, III (Autumn 1957), 216–224.

———. "The Church and Major Scobie," *Renascence*, X (Spring 1958), 115–120.

———. "The Entertaining Mr. Greene," *Renascence*, XIV (Autumn 1961), 8–24.

———. "Greene's *The Comedians*: Hollower Men," *Renascence*, XVIII (1966), 129–136, 146.

———. "Notes on *The Power and the Glory*," *The Annotator*, no. 5 (May 1955), pp. 7–10.

———. "The Religious Theme in the Novels of Rex Warner, Evelyn Waugh, and Graham Greene," *Dissertation Abstracts*, XV (1955), 605–606.

Didion, J. "Marks of Identity," *National Review*, X (March 25, 1961), 190–191.

Dinkins, Paul. "Graham Greene: The Incomplete Version," *Catholic World*, CLXXVI (November 1952), 96–102.

Dooley, D. J. "*A Burnt-Out Case* Reconsidered," *Wiseman Review*, CCXXXVII (Summer 1963), 168–178.

———. "The Suspension of Disbelief: Greene's *Burnt-Out Case*," *Dalhousie Review*, XLIII (Autumn 1963), 343–352.

Downing, Francis. "The Art of Fiction," *Commonweal*, LV (December 28, 1951), 297–298.

———. "Graham Greene and the Case for Disloyalty," *Commonweal*, LV (March 14, 1952), 564–566.

Doyle, L. F. "Graham Greene as Moralist," *America*, XCI (September 18, 1954), 604.

Duché, Jean. "Je n'écrivai plus de romans policiers, nous dit Graham Greene," *Figaro Littéraire*, (December 20, 1947), p. 6.

———. "Du Rocher de Sysyphe au Rocher de Brighton," *La Table Ronde*, no. 2 (February 1948), pp. 306–309.

Duesberg, Jacques. "Un épigone du 'Misérabilisme': Graham Greene," *Synthèses*, no. 69 (February 1952), pp. 348–353.

Duffy, Joseph M., Jr. "The Lost World of Graham Greene," *Thought*, XXXIII (Summer 1958), 229–247.

Du Parc, Robert. "Saint ou maudit? Le prêtre dans 'La Puissance et la Gloire,' " *Etudes*, CCLX (March 1949), 368–381.

Duprey, Richard A. "Morris West, A Witness for Compassion," *Catholic World*, CXCIII (September 1961), 360–366.

Eishiskina, N. "Graham Greene's Novels," *Voprosi Literaturi*, VI (June 1961), 149–169.

Elistratova, Anna. "Graham Greene and His New Novel," *Soviet Literature*, VIII (1956), 149–155.

Ellis, William D., Jr. "The Grand Theme of Graham Greene," *Southwest Review*, XLI (Summer 1956), 239–250.

Elsen, Claude. "Graham Greene ou la geste de l'homme traque," *La Table Ronde*, no. 14 (February 1949), pp. 297–301.

Engel, Claire Elaine. "Einige Englische Romanciers von Heute," *Du*, VIII (January 1948), 28.

Engelborghs, Maurits. "Dagboek van een romancier," *Dietsche Warande en Belfort*, CVII (1962), 372.

———. "De Nieuwe Roman van Graham Greene," *Kultuurleven*, XXVI (February 1959), 119–122.

———. "De opuatting van roman en romanschrijver bij Graham Greene," *Dietsche Warande en Belfort*, CIX (1964), 172–198.

———. "Engelse Letteren: *The Complaisant Lover*: Een Blijspel van Graham Greene," *Dietsche Warande en Belfort*, no. 8 (October 1959), pp. 497–501.

———. "Engelse Letteren: Graham Greene: 'The Potting Shed,' " *Dietsche Warande en Belfort*, V (1958), 306–310.

———. "Graham Greene," *Dietsche Warande en Belfort*, IV (1957), 234–239.

———. "Graham Greene: *A Burnt-Out Case*," *Kultuurleven*, XXVIII (October 1961), 610–615.

———. "Graham Greene op de terugweg?" *Dietsche Warande en Belfort*, CIX (1964), 55–63.

Erba, Luciano. "Incontro con Graham Greene,"*Vita e Pensiero*, XXXII (September 1949), 507–509.

Evans, Robert O. "Existentialism in Graham Greene's *The Quiet American*," *Modern Fiction Studies*, III (Autumn 1957), 241–248.

Fadiman, Clifton. "The Decline of Attention," *Saturday Review of Literature*, XXXII (August 6, 1949), 20–24.

Fielding, Gabriel. "Graham Greene: The Religious Englishman," *Listener*, LXXII (September 24, 1964), 465–466.

Findlater, Richard. "Graham Greene as Dramatist," *Twentieth Century*, CLVI (June 1953), 471–473.

Flint, R. W. "Recent Fiction," *Hudson Review*, I (1948–1949), 590–596.

Flood, Ethelbert, O. F. M. "Christian Language in Modern Literature," *Culture*, XII (1961), 28–42.

Folk, Barbara Nauer. "Fiction: A Problem for the Catholic Writer," *Catholic World*, CLXXXVIII (November 1958), 105–109.

Fouchet, Max-Pol. "Graham Greene," *Revue de Paris*, LVII (July 1950), 59–68.

Fowler, Alastair. "Novelist of Damnation," *Theology*, (July 1953), pp. 259–264.

Freedman, Ralph. "Novel of Contention: *The Quiet American*," *Western Review*, XXI (Autumn 1956), 76–81.

Fremantle, Anne. "The Hunted Men of Graham Greene," *Saturday Review*, XXXVI (January 10, 1953), 15–16.

Fytton, Francis. "Graham Greene: Catholicism and Controversy," *Catholic World*, CLXXX (December 1954), 172–175.

Gainham, S. "Grim Grin," *Spectator*, CCX (May 31, 1963), 694.

Gardiner, Harold C. "Graham Greene, Catholic Shocker," *Renascence*, I (Spring 1949), 12–15.

———. "Nature and Grace," *America*, XCIV (March 10, 1956), 639.

———. "Taste and Worth," *America*, LXXV (April 20, 1946), 53.

Garrigue, Jean. "Six Writers of Crisis," *Commentary*, XXVII (March 1959), 270–272.

Gassner, John. "Broadway in Review," *Educational Theatre Journal*, XI (March 1959), 29–39.

Glicksberg, Charles I. "Graham Greene: Catholicism in Fiction," *Criticism*, I (Fall 1959), 339–353.

Göller, Karl Heinz. "Graham Greene: *The Power and the Glory*," *Der moderne englische Roman*, (1966), pp. 245–261.

Gonzalez Salas, Carlos. "Tres libros y tres autores discutidos: Graham Greene contra Mejico," *Abside*, XXIV (1960), 358–361.

Gordon, Caroline. "Some Readings and Misreadings," *Sewanee Review*, LXI (Summer 1953), 393–396.

Graef, Hilda. "Marriage and Our Catholic Novelists," *Catholic World*, CLXXXIX (June 1959), 185–190.

Graude, Luke. "Gabriel Fielding, New Master of the Catholic Classic?" *Catholic World*, CXCVII (June 1964), 172–179.

Gregor, Ian. "The Greene Baize Door," *Blackfriars*, XXXVI (September 1955), 327–333.

———. "The New Romanticism: A Comment on 'The Living Room,' " *Blackfriars*, XXXIV (September 1953), 403–406.

Grenzmann, Wilhelm. "Das Leiden der Literatur—Das Leiden an der Literatur," *Begegnung*, XIX (July–August 1964), 5–10.

Grubbs, Henry A. "Albert Camus and Graham Greene," *Modern Language Quarterly*, X (March 1949), 33–42.

Grunt, Olav Paus. "Grunntrekk i Graham Greenes Fortellerkunst," *Samtiden*, LXIII (1954), 341–349.

Gusdorf, Barbara Neuroth. "Concepts of Sainthood in the Novels of Albert Camus and Graham Greene," *Dissertation Abstracts*, XXIX (1968), 1895A–1896A.

Haber, Herbert R. "The Two Worlds of Graham Greene," *Modern Fiction Studies*, III (Autumn 1957), 256–268.

Hahn, Karl J. "Graham Greene," *Hochland* (München), XLI (July 1959), 455–465.

Happel, Nikolaus. "Formbetrachtung an Graham Greens Short Story 'The Hint of an Explanaiton,' " *Die Neueren Sprachen*, (1960), pp. 81–86.

Harmer, Ruth Mulvey. "Greene World of Mexico: The Birth of a Novelist," *Renascence*, XV (1963), 171–182, 194.

Hayes, H. R. "A Defense of the Thriller," *Partisan Review*, XII (Winter 1945), 135–137.

Hayman, Ronald. "Le Roman Anglais d'Après-Guerre, III," *Revue de lettres modernes*, III (April 1954), 88–93.

Herling, Gutav. "Two Sanctities: Greene and Camus," *Adam*, no. 201 (December 1949), pp. 10–19.

Herzog, Bert. "Welt unter geschlossenem Himmel, zu de Büchern von Graham Greene," *Stimmen der Zeit*, CLI (March 1952), 420–426 and (October 1952), 20–25.

Hess, M. W. "Greene's Travesty on 'The Ring and the Book,' " *Catholic World*, CXCIV (October 1961), 37–42.

Hewes, Henry. "Resurrection Will Out," *Saturday Review*, XL (February 16, 1957), 26–27.

Hicks, Granville. "Gestation of a Brain Child," *Saturday Review*, XLV (January 6, 1962), 62.

———. "In a Novel It's the Life, Not the Politics, That Counts," *New York Times Book Review*, (August 12, 1956), 5.

Highet, Gilbert. "Our Man in Purgatory," *Horizon*, III (May 1961), 116–117.

Hillig, Franz, S. J. "Die Kraft und die Herrlichkeit," *Stimmen der Zeit* (Freiburg), CXLIII (February 1949), 354–366.

Hinchliffe, A. P. "Good American," *Twentieth Century*, CLXVIII (December 1960), 529–539.

Hobson, L. Z. "Innocent Abroad," *Good Housekeeping*, CXVII (March 1956), 13.

Hoggart, Richard. "The Force of Caricature: Aspects of the Art of Graham Greene, with Particular Reference to *The Power and the Glory*," *Essays in Criticism*, III (October 1953), 447–462.

Hollis, Carroll C. "Nathanael West and the 'Lonely Crowd,'" *Thought*, XXXIII (Autumn 1958), 398–416.

Horst, Karl August. "Argernis der Schöptung, zur Theologie Graham Greenes," *Merkur*, V (February 1951), 184–187.

Hortmann, Wilhelm. "Graham Greene: The Burnt-Out Catholic," *Twentieth Century Literature*, X (1964), 64–76.

Howes, Jane. "Out of the Pit," *Catholic World*, CLXXI (April 1950), 36–40.

Hughes, Catharine. "Innocence Revisited," *Renascence*, XII (Autumn 1959), 29–34.

Hughes, R. E. "*The Quiet American*: The Case Reopened," *Renascence*, XII (Autumn 1959), 41–42, 49.

Igoe, W. J. "Graham Greene," *John O'London's*, IV (June 6, 1961), 24–25.

———. "London Letter," *America*, XCII (December 23, 1954), 99–101.

Ihlenfeld, Kurt. "Kann ein Sünder ein Heiliger sein?" *Evangelische Welt* (Bethel), III (1947), 636.

Ivaschova, Valentina. "Legende und Wahrheit über Graham Greene," *Zeitschrift für Anglistik und Amerikanistik*, X (1962), 229–258.

Jacobsen, Josephine. "A Catholic Quartet," *Christian Scholar*, XLVII (Summer 1964), 139–154.

Jameson, Storm. "British Literature: Survey and Critique," *Saturday Review*, XXXIV (October 13, 1951), 24–26, 47.

Jans, Adrien. "Graham Greene, entre le péché et l'amour," *Empreintes*, IV (February–April 1948), 46–49.

Jefferson, Mary Evelyn. "*The Heart of the Matter*: The Responsible Man," *Carolina Quarterly*, IX (Summer 1957), 23–31.

Jerrold, Douglas. "Graham Greene, Pleasure-Hater," *Harper's*, CCV (August 1952), 50–52. Also printed in *Picture Post*, LIV (March 15, 1952), 51–53.

Johnston, J. L. "Graham Greene—The Unhappy Man," *The Central Literary Magazine* (Birmingham), XXXVIII (July 1954), 43–49.

Jones, James Land. "Graham Greene and the Structure of the Moral Imagination," *Phoenix*, no. 2 (1966), pp. 34–56.

Joseph, Brother, F. S. C. "Greene's 'The Hint of an Explanation,' " *The Explicator*, XIX (January 1961), no. 21.

Jouve, Raymond. "La Damnation de Scobie?" *Etudes*, no. 263 (November 1949), pp. 164–177.

Kauffman, Stanley. "With Graham Greene in Havana," *New Republic*, CXLII (February 15, 1960), 22–23.

Kelleher, James P. "The Orthodoxy and Values of Graham Greene," *Dissertation Abstracts*, XXVII (1966), 1825A.

Kenny, Herbert A. "Graham Greene," *Catholic World*, CLXXXV (August 1957), 326–329.

Kermode, Frank. "Mr. Green's Eggs and Crosses," *Encounter*, XVI (April 1961), 69–75.

———. "The House of Fiction: Interview with Seven English Novelists," *Partisan Review*, XXX (Spring 1963), 61–82.

Kevin, Neil. "Fiction Priests," *Irish Ecclesiastical Record*, LX (October 1940), 253–257.

Khatchadourian, Haig. "Some Major Trends in Twentieth-Century English Literature," *Visva-Bharati Quarterly*, XXVII (Autumn 1961), 140–149.

King, Bruce. "Graham Greene's Inferno," *Etudes Anglaises*, XXI (1968), 35–51.

Kunitz, Stanley J., ed. *Twentieth Century Authors*, 1st Supplement, New York: Wilson, 1955, pp. 387–388.

Kunkel, Francis Leo. "A Critical Study of Graham Greene," *Dissertation Abstracts*, XX (1959), 670–671.

———. "The Priest as Scapegoat in the Modern Catholic Novel," *Ramparts*, I (January 1963), 72–78.

Lanina, T. "Paradoxes of Graham Greene," *Inostrannaja Literatura*, III (March 1959), 188–196.

Las Vergnas, Raymond. "A Propos de Graham Greene," *Hommes et Mondes*, IX (May 1949), 147–151.

Laurens, A. "Comment j'ai introduit Graham Greene in France," *France-Asie* (Saigon), III (April 1948), 455–459.

Lees, F. N. "Graham Greene: A Comment," *Scrutiny*, XIX (October 1952), 31–42.

Lehmann, J. "The Blundering, Ineffectual American," *New Republic*, CXXXIV (March 12, 1956), 26–27.

Lerner, Lawrence. "Graham Greene," *Critical Quarterly*, V (Autumn 1963), 217–231.

Lewis, R. W. B. "The Fiction of Graham Greene: Between the Horror and the Glory," *Kenyon Review*, XIX (Winter 1957), 56–75.

———. "The 'Trilogy' of Graham Greene," *Modern Fiction Studies*, III (Autumn 1957), 195–215.

Liebling, A. J. "Talkative Something-or-Other," *New Yorker*, XXXII (April 7, 1956), 148–154.

Lindman-Stafford, Kerstin. "En sorts komedi," *Horisont* (Vasa), XIII (1966), 27–30. (On *The Comedians*.)

Lodge, David. "Graham Greene's Comedians," *Commonweal*, LXXXIII (1966), 604–606.

———. "Use of Key Words in the Novels of Graham Greene: Love, Hate, and *The End of the Affair*," *Blackfriars*, XLII (November 1961), 468–474.

Lohf, Kenneth A. "Graham Greene and the Problem of Evil," *Catholic World*, CLXXIII (June 1951), 196–199.

McCall, Dan. "*Brighton Rock*: The Price of Order," *English Language Notes*, III (1966), 290–294.

McCarthy, Mary. "Graham Greene and the Intelligentsia," *Partisan Review*, XI (Spring 1944), 228–230.

McCormick, John O. "The Rough and Lurid Vision: Henry James, Graham Greene and the International Theme," *Jahrbuch für Amerikastudien*, II (1957), 158–167.

McDonnell, Lawrence V. "The Priest-Hero in the Modern Novel," *Catholic World*, CXCVI (February 1963), 306–311.

McGowan, F. A. "Symbolism in *Brighton Rock*," *Renascence*, VIII (Autumn 1955), 25–35.

McLaughlin, R. "Graham Greene: Saint or Cynic?" *America*, LXXIX (July 24, 1948), 370–371.

———. "I've Been Reading . . . ," *Theatre Arts*, XXXV (December 1951), 34–35.

McMahon, J. "Graham Green and *The Quiet American*," *Jammu and Kashmir University Review*, I (November 1958), 64–73.

McNamara, E. "Prospects of the Catholic Novel," *America*, XCVII (August 17, 1957), 505–506.

Magill, Frank N., ed. *Cyclopedia of World Authors*, New York: Harper, 1958, pp 454–457.

Magny, Claude-Edmonde. "De Benito Cereno au Rocher de Brighton," *Guilde du Livre*, XVI (July 1951), 150–153.

———. "Graham Greene," *Poésie 46*, no. 32 (May 1946), pp. 32–37.

Maguire, C. E. "Grace and the Play," *America*, XCIII (July 30, 1955), 433–435.

Marian, Sister, I. H. M. "Graham Greene's People: Being and Becoming," *Renascence*, XVIII (1965), 19–22.

Markovic, Vida E. "Graham Greene in Search of God," *Texas Studies in Literature and Language*, V (Summer 1963), 271–282.

Marshall, Bruce. "Graham Greene and Evelyn Waugh," *Commonweal*, LI (March 3, 1950), 551–553.

Mason, H. A. "A Note on Contemporary 'Philosophical' Literary Criticism in France," *Scrutiny*, XVI (March 1949), 54–60.

Mauriac, François. "La Puissance et la Gloire," *Renascence*, I (Spring 1949), 25–27. Also printed in *Figaro Litéraire*, (October 30, 1948), pp. 1, 3.

Maurois, André. "Points of View," *Ungar*, (1968), pp. 381–409.

Maxwell, J. C. " 'The Dry Salvages': A Possible Echo of Graham Greene," *Notes and Queries*, XI (October 1964), 387.

Mayne, Richard. "Where God Makes the Scenery," *New Statesman*, LXVI (August 2, 1963), 144.

Mesnet, M. B. "Le 'Potting Shed' de Graham Greene," *Etudes*, CCXCVI (September 1958), 238–247.

Michener, Richard L. "Apocalyptic Mexico: *The Plumed Serpent* and *The Power and the Glory*," *University Review* (Kansas City), XXXIV (June 1968), 313–316.

Miller, Bruce. "Graham Greene," *Meanjin*, V (Spring 1946), 193–197.

Mondrone, Domenico, S. I. "Uno Sguardo su Graham Greene da l'*Ultima Stanza*," *Civiltà Cattolica*, Anno 108, II (May 1957), 279–293.

Monroe, N. Elizabeth. "The New Man in Fiction," *Renascence*, VI (August 1953), 9–17.

Montesi, Gotthard. "Tragödie der Nächstenliebe," *Wort und Wahrheit*, III (August 1948), 610–615.

Moré, Marcel. "A Propos de Newman," *Dieu Vivant*, no. 15 (1950), pp. 63–81.

———, and Père Jouve. "Propos de Table avec Graham Greene," *Dieu Vivant*, no. 16 (1950), pp. 127–137.

———. "The Two Holocausts of Scobie," *Cross Currents*, I (1951), 44–63. Also as "Les Deux Holocaustes de Scobie," *Dieu Vivant*, no. 16 (1950), pp. 77–105.

Murphy, John P., S. J. " 'The Potting Shed,' " *Renascence*, XII (Autumn 1959), 43–49.

Neis, Edgar. "Zum Sprachstil Graham Greenes," *Die Neueren Sprachen*, (April 1957), pp. 166–173.

Nicholson, Jenny. "Graham Greene—A Third Man of Real Life," *Picture Post*, LXIV (August 14, 1954), 18–19.

North, Roy. "Graham Greene," *Visva-bharati Quarterly*, XXI (Spring 1956), 376–399.

Noxon, James. "Kierkegaard's Stages and *A Burnt-Out Case*," *Review of English Literature*, III (January 1962), 90–101.

O'Donnell, Donat. "Graham Greene's Lost Childhood," *A. D. 52*, III (Winter 1952), 43–47.

O'Donovan, P. "Graham Greene's Leper Colony," *New Republic*, CXLIV (February 20, 1961), 21–22.

O'Faolain, Sean. "The Novels of Graham Greene: *The Heart of the Matter*," *Britain To-day*, no. 148 (August 1948), pp. 32–36.

O'Grady, Emmett. "Graham Greene, écrivain eschatologique," *Revue de l'Université d'Ottawa*, XXII (April 1952), 156–170.

Osterman, Robert. "Interview with Graham Greene," *Catholic World*, CLXX (February 1950), 356–361.

Paleivskij, P. "Fantomy: Buržuaznyj mir v romanax Grema Grina," *Nouyj mir*, XXXVIII, no. 6 (1962), pp. 229–243.

Parinaud, André. "La Leçon de Vengeance de Graham Greene," *Arts*, no. 565 (April 25, 1956), pp. 1, 6.

Parsons, L. "Graham Greene," *Fortnightly*, CLXXVI (October 1951), 704–705.

Patten, Karl. "The Structure of *The Power and the Glory*," *Modern Fiction Studies*, III (Autumn 1957), 225–234.

Peters, S. J. "*A Burnt-Out Case*, Een mislukte roman," *Streven*, (November 1961), pp. 161–166.

Peters, W. "The Concern of Graham Greene," *The Month*, X (November 1953), 281–290.

Pfleger, Karl. "Religiöse Wirklichkeit . . . ," *Wort und Wahrheit*, IV (June 1949), 473–478.

Phillips, W. "The Pursuit of Good and Evil," *American Mercury*, LXXIV (May 1952), 102–106.

Pitts, Arthur W., Jr. "Greene's 'The Basement Room,' " *Explicator*, XXIII (October 1964), no. 17.

Powell, Dilys. "A Trio of Thrillers," *Britain To-Day*, no. 178 (February 1951), p. 36.

Pritchett, V. S. "It's a Battlefield," *Spectator*, CLII (1934), 206.

———. "The World of Graham Greene," *New Statesman*, LV (January 4, 1958), 17–18.

Puentevella, Renato, S. J. "Ambiguity in Greene," *Renascence*, XII (Autumn 1959), 35–37.

Rahv, Philip. "Wicked American Innocence," *Commentary*, XXI (May 1956), 488–490.

Pujals, Esteban. "The Globe Theatre, Londres," *Filologia moderna*, I (1960), 59–63.

Remords, G. "Graham Greene: Notes Biographiques et Bibliographiques," *Bulletin de la Faculté des Lettres de Strasbourg*, XXIX (May–June 1951), 393–399.

Rewak, W. J. " 'The Potting Shed,' Maturation of Graham Greene's Vision," *Catholic World*, CLXXXVI (December 1957), 210–213.

Rimaud, Jean. "Psychologists versus Morality," *Cross Currents*, no. 2 (1951), pp. 26–38.

Robertson, Roderick. "Toward a Definition of Religious Drama," *Educational Theatre Journal*, IX (1957), 99–105.

Rodriguez Monegal, Emir. " 'El Revés de la Trama' o la Màscara del Realismo," *Sur*, no. 183 (January 1950), pp. 57–60.

Rolo, Charles J. "Graham Greene: The Man and the Message," *Atlantic Monthly*, CCVII (May 1961), 60–65.

Rosewald, Robert. "Graham Greene op nieuwe paden," *De Periscoop*, (February 1, 1956), p. 7.

Rostenne, Paul. "Introduction à Graham Greene: Romancier Catholique," *Revue Nouvelle*, VI (September 15, 1947), 193–204.

Roy, Jean-Henri. "L'oeuvre de Graham Greene ou un christianisme de la damnation," *Les Temps Modernes*, V (1950), 1513–1519.

Rudman, Harry W. "Clough and Graham Greene's *The Quiet American*," *Victorian Newsletter*, no. 19 (1961), pp. 14–15.

Ruotolo, Lucia P. "*Brighton Rock*'s Absurd Heroine," *Modern Language Quarterly*, XXV (1964), 425–433.

Sackville-West, Edward. "The Electric Hare: Some Aspects of Graham Greene," *The Month*, VI (September 1951), 141–147.

———. "Time-Bomb," *The Month*, XXV (March 1961), 175–178.

Sandra, Sister Mary, S. S. A. "The Priest-Hero in Modern Fiction," *The Personalist*, XLVI (1965), 527–542.

Schmidthüs, Karlheinz. "Graham Greenes Katholizismus: Die religiöse Erfahrung der Welt in seinem Romanen," *Wort und Wahrheit*, XII (January 1957), 39–51.

Schoonderwoerd, N. "Heeft Graham Greene Ons Weer Teleurgesteld?" *Kultuurleven*, XXVI (November 1959), 703–704.

Schumann, Hildegard. "Zum Problem des Anti-Helden in Graham Greenes neueren Romanen," *Wissenschaftliche Zeitschrift der Universität Romstock*, XII (1963), 71–77.

Scott, Nathan A., Jr. "Christian Novelist's Dilemma," *Christian Century*, LXXIII (August 1, 1956), 901–902.

Servotte, Herman. "Bedenkingen bij *A Burnt-Out Case*, Graham Greene's jongste roman," *Dietsche Warande en Belfort*, CVI (June 1961), 371–375.

———. "Bij de jongste roman van Graham Greene." *Dietsche Warande en Belfort*, VI (1955), 367-370.

Seward, Barbara. "Graham Greene: A Hint of an Explanation," *Western Review*, XXII (Winter 1958), 83–95.

Sewell, Elizabeth. "Graham Greene," *Dublin Review*, CCXXVII (First Quarter 1954), 12–21.

———. "The Imagination of Graham Greene," *Thought*, XXIX (March 1954), 51–60.

Sheed, Wilfrid. "Enemies of Catholic Promise," *Commonweal*, LXXVII (1963), 560–563.

Shuttleworth, Martin, and Simon Raven. "The Art of Fiction: III. Graham Greene," *Paris Review*, I (Autumn 1953), 24–41.

Siecke, Gerda. "Das Romanwerk Graham Greenes in seinem Verhaltnis zu den Romanen van Georges Bernanos und François Mauriac," Master's dissertation, Erlangen, 1955.

Silva Delgado, Adolfo. "La Carrera literaria de Graham Greene," *Marcha*, XIII (November 23, 1951), 14–15, 71.

Silveira, Gerald E. "Greene's 'The Basement Room,' " *Explicator*, XV (December 1965), no. 13.

Simon, John K. "Off the *Voie royale*: The Failure of Greene's *A Burnt-Out Case*," *Symposium*, XVIII (1964), 163–169.

Simons, J. W. "Salvation in the Novels," *Commonweal*, LVI (April 25, 1952), 74–76.

Simons, Katherine. "Graham Greene," *Book-of-the-Month-Club News*, June 1948, pp. 6–7.

Slate, Audrey Nelson. "Technique and Form in the Novels of Graham Greene," *Dissertation Abstracts*, XXI (1960), 629–630.

Smith, A. J. M. "Graham Greene's Theological Thrillers," *Queen's Quarterly*, LXVIII (Spring 1961), 15–33.

Smith, Francis J. "The Anatomy of *A Burnt-Out Case*," *America*, CV (September 9, 1961), 711–712.

Sordet, Etienne. "Signification de Graham Greene," *Cahiers Protestants*, XXXVII (1953), 239–250.

Spaventa Filippi, Lia. "Produzione poliziesca di Graham Greene," *L'Italia che scrive*, XLV (1962), 87.

Spier, Ursula. "Melodrama in Graham Greene's *The End of the Affair*," *Modern Fiction Studies*, III (Autumn 1957), 235–240.

Spinnucci, Pietro. "L'ultimo dramma di Graham Greene," *Humanitas* (Brescia), XV (1960), 820–825.

Stanford, Derek. " 'The Potting Shed,' " *Contemporary Review*, no. 1110 (June 1958), pp. 301-303.

Stanley, John. "Life in the Living Room," *Commonweal*, LXI (December 31, 1954), 354–355.

Sternlicht, Sanford. "The Sad Comedies: Graham Greene's Later Novels," *Florida Quarterly*, I (1968), 65–77.

Stratford, Philip. "Chalk and Cheese: A Comparative Study of *A Kiss for the Leper* and *A Burnt-Out Case*," *University of Toronto Quarterly*, XXXIII (January 1964), 200–218.

———. "Graham Greene: Master of Melodrama," *Tamarack Review*, no. 19 (Spring 1961), pp. 67–86.

———. "The Uncomplacent Dramatist: Some Aspects of Graham Greene's Theatre," *Wisconsin Studies in Contemporary Literature*, II (Fall 1961), 5–19.

———. "Unlocking the Potting Shed," *Kenyon Review*, XXIV (Winter 1962), 129–143.

Sullivan, Dan. "The Theater: Graham Greene's 'Carving a Statue,' " *The New York Times*, CXVII (May 1, 1968), 43.

Sultan, Stanley. "An Old-Irish Model for *Ulysses*," *James Joyce Quarterly*, V (1968), 103–109.

Sylvester, Harry. "Graham Greene," *Commonweal,* XXXIII (October 25, 1940), 11–13.

Taber, Robert. "Castro's Cuba," *Nation*, CXC (January 23, 1960), 63–64.

Tarnawski, Wit. "Przemiany Graham Greene's," *Kultura*, no. 138 (April 1959), pp. 131–137.

Taylor, Marion A., and John Clark. "Further Sources for 'The Second Death' by Graham Greene," *Papers on English Language and Literature*, I (1965), 378–380.

Toynbee, Philip. "Literature and Life—2: Graham Greene on 'The Job of the Writer,' " *Observer*, (September 15, 1957), p. 3.

Tracy, Honor. "Life and Soul of the Party," *New Republic*, CXL (April 20 ,1959), 15–16.

———. "Two Voices Are There," *New Republic*, CXLVI (February 5, 1962), 20–21.

Traversi, Derek. "Graham Greene: I. The Earlier Novels. II. The Later Novels," *Twentieth Century*, CXLIX (March 1951), 231–240; CXLIX (April 1951), 318–328.

Tressin, Deanna. "Toward Understanding," *English Journal*, LV (1966), 1170–1174.

Trilling, Diana, and Philip Rhav. "America and *The Quiet American*," *Commentary*, XXII (July 1956), 66–71.

Turnell, Martin. "The Religious Novel," *Commonweal*, LV (October 26, 1951), 55–57.

Tynan, Kenneth. "An Inner View of Graham Greene," *Harper's Bazaar*, LXXXVI (February 1953), 128–129, 209–210, 214–215. Abridged in *Persona Grata* (London: Wingate, 1953), pp. 53–56.

Tysdahl, Bjørn. "Graham Greene—fluktens og forfølgelsens dikter," *Kirke og Kultur*, LXVII (1962), 293–298.

Viatte, A. "Graham Greene, Romancier de la Grâce," *Revue de l'Université Laval*, IV (April 1950), 753–758.

Vieira, Manuel. "Notas para um estudo sobre Graham Greene," *Tempo presente*, no. 20 (1960), pp. 46–52.

Voorhees, Richard J. "Recent Greene," *South Atlantic Quarterly*, LXII (Spring 1963), 244–255.

———. "The World of Graham Greene," *South Atlantic Quarterly*, L (July 1951), 389–398.

Walbridge, E. "Letter Discussing Graham Greene and Beatrix Potter," *Saturday Review of Literature*, XXVII (February 12, 1944), 36.

Wall, Barbara. "London Letter," *America*, LXXIX (August 28, 1948), 470–471.

Walters, Dorothy Jeanne. "The Theme of Destructive Innocence in the Modern Novel: Greene, James, Cary, Porter," *Dissertation Abstracts*, XXI (February 1961), 2300–2301.

Wansbrough, John. "Graham Greene: The Detective in the Wasteland," *Harvard Advocate*, CXXXVI (December 1952), 11–13, 29–31.

Wassmer, Thomas A. "Faith and Belief: A Footnote to Greene's *Visit to Morin*," *Renascence*, XI (1959), 84–88.

———. "*Faith and Reason* in Graham Greene,"*Studies* [An Irish Quarterly Review], XLVIII (Summer 1959), 163–167.

———. "Graham Greene: A Look at His Sinners," *Critic*, XVIII (December 1959–January 1960), 16–17, 72–74.

———, "Graham Greene: Literary Artist and Philosopher-Theologian," *Homiletic and Pastoral Review*, LVIII (March 1958), 583–589.

———. "The Problem and Mystery of Sin in the Works of Graham Greene," *The Christian Scholar*, XLIII (Winter 1960), 309–315.

———. "Reason and Faith as Seen by Graham Greene," *Drama Critique*, II (November 1959), 126–130.

———. "The Sinners of Graham Greene," *Dalhousie Review*, XXXIX (Autumn 1959), 326–332.

Wasson, John. "Hamlet's Second Chance," *Research Studies* (Washington State University), XXVIII (September 1960), 117–124.

Waugh, Evelyn. "Felix Culpa?" *Commonweal*, XLVIII (July 16, 1948), 322–325. Also printed in *Tablet*, CXCI June 5, 1948), 352–354.

———. "The Heart's Own Reasons," *Commonweal*, LIV (August 17, 1951), 458–459. Also printed in *The Month*, VI (September 1951), 174–176.

West, Anthony. "Saint's Progress," *New Yorker*, XXVII (November 10, 1951), 154.

Weyergans, Franz. "*La Saison Des Pluies* de Graham Greene," *Revue Nouvelle*, XXXIII (April 1961), 417–420.

Wichert, Robert A. "The Quality of Graham Greene's Mercy," *College English*, XXV (November 1963), 99–103.

Woodcock, George. "Mexico and the English Novelists," *Western Review*, XXI (Autumn 1956), 21–32.

Wright, Andrew. "A Note on Joyce Cary's Reputation," *Modern Fiction Studies*, IX (Autumn 1963), 207–209.

Young, Vernon. "Hell on Earth: Six Versions," *Hudson Review*, II (Summer 1949), 311–317.

Zabel, M. D. "Graham Greene," *Nation*, CLVII (July 3, 1943), 18–20.

Unsigned. "Adam's Tree," *Twentieth Century*, CL (October 1951), 334–342.

Unsigned. "Américain tranquille," *Nouvelles Littéraires*, (March 8, 1956), p. 7.

Unsigned. "The Angry Man Within (An Interview)," *Sunday Times* [London], April 12, 1953, p. 5.

Unsigned. Biographical Note, *Publisher's Weekly*, CLXIII (January 3, 1953), 30.

Unsigned. Biographical Note, *Saturday Review of Literature*, XXXI (July 10, 1948), 9.

Unsigned. Biographical Note, *Time*, LII (August 9, 1948), 85.

Unsigned. Biographical Note, *Wilson Bulletin*, IV (November 1929), 98.

Unsigned. "Colette's Burial," *Commonweal*, LX (September 17, 1954), 573.

Unsigned. "Diem's Critics; Graham Greene and Father O'Conner's Reply," *America*, XCIII (May 28, 1955), 225.

Unsigned. "Engelse letteren: Beschouwingen bij de laatste roman van Graham Greene," *Dietsche Warande en Belfort*, (1956), pp. 433–444.

Unsigned. "Graham Green vs. Selwyn Lloyd," *Time and Tide*, XL (January 17, 1959), 65.

Unsigned. "Greene, Not Red," *Newsweek*, XXXIX (February 11, 1952), 28.

Unsigned. "The Greeneland Aboriginal," *New Statesman*, LXI (January 13, 1961), 44–45.

Unsigned. "Greene's Disservice to Church," *America*, XCIV (February 11, 1956), 518.

Unsigned. "Group Loyalties," *Times Literary Supplement* [London], January 15, 1949, p. 41.

Unsigned. "The Lady Vanishes, But What's Become of her Daughters?" *Times Literary Supplement* [London], September 9, 1960, p. lix.

Unsigned. "Men Who Fascinate Women," *Look*, XIX (September 6, 1955), 43.

Unsigned. "Mr. Greene Promises No More Miracles," *Life*, XLII (April 1, 1957), 68.

Unsigned. "New Honor and New Novel," *Life*, LX (February 4, 1960), 43–44.

Unsigned. "New Year's Honours," *London Illustrated News*, CCXLVIII (January 8, 1966), 13.

Unsigned. "Novelist Graham Greene: Adultery Can Lead to Sainthood," *Time*, LVIII (October 29, 1951), 98–104.

Unsigned. "Profile—Graham Greene," *Observer*, November 27, 1949, p. 2.

Unsigned. "Propros de table avec Graham Greene," *Dieu Vivant*, no. 16 (1950), pp. 127–137.

Unsigned. "Shocker," *Time*, LVIII (October 29, 1951), 98–104.

Unsigned. "This is Graham Greene," *Newsweek*, XLIV (November 29, 1954), 92–93.

Unsigned. "To Get Rave Reviews, Write an Anti-U.S.A. Novel!" *Saturday Evening Post*, CCXXIX (October 6, 1956), 10.

Unsigned. "When Greene Is Red," *Newsweek*, XLVIII (October 1, 1956), 94, 96.

Unsigned. "Whose Man in Havana?" *Commonweal*, LXX (July 3, 1959), 342.

E. Greene's Novels: A Chronological Listing With Reviews

The Man Within. London: Heinemann, 1929.

REVIEWS:

Allen, Paul. *Bookman*, LXX (December 29, 1929), 449.

Baird, Enid. *New York Herald Tribune*, October 20, 1929, p. 23.

Brebner, Bartlet. *Saturday Review of Literature*, VI (October 19, 1929), 287.

Codman, Florence. *Nation*, CXXIX (October 23, 1929), 468.

Robbins, F. L. *Outlook*, CLIII (December 25, 1929), 670.

Thomas, Gilbert. *Spectator*, CXLII (June 22, 1929), 982.

Unsigned. *Boston Transcript*, November 13, 1929, p. 5.

Unsigned. *Nation and Anthenaeum*, XLV (August 3, 1929), 602.

Unsigned. *Times Literary Supplement* [London], June 20, 1929, p. 492.

The Name of Action. London: Heinemann, 1930.

REVIEWS:

Footner, Hulbert. *Saturday Review of Literature*, VII (March 14, 1931), 664.

Robbins, F. L. *Outlook*, CLVII (March 11, 1931), 374.

Sykes, Gerald. *Books*, February 15, 1931, p. 18.

Tomlinson, K. C. *Nation and Athenaeum*, XLVIII (November 15, 1930), 242.

Walton, Edith H. *The New York Times Book Review*, Section IV, March 8, 1931, p. 7.

Unsigned. *Booklist*, XXVII (May 1931), 407.

Unsigned. *Bookman*, LXXIII (April 1931), 195.

Unsigned. *Boston Transcript*, February 25, 1931, p. 3.

Unsigned. *Forum*, LXXXV (May 1931), 16.

Unsigned. *The Times [London]*, October 7, 1930, p. 8e.

Unsigned. *New Republic*, LXVI (March 18, 1931), 135.

Unsigned. *New Statesman*, XXXVI (November 8, 1930), 148.

Unsigned. *Times Literary Supplement* [London], October 9, 1930, p. 804.

Rumor at Nightfall. London: Heinemann, 1931.

REVIEWS:

Bullett, Gerald. *New Statesman and Nation*, II (November 14, 1931), 614.

Cantwell, Robert. *New York Evening Post*, January 30, 1932, p. 9.

Unsigned. *Forum*, LXXXVII (April 1932), 11.

Unsigned. *Nation*, CXXXIV (May 18, 1932), 578.

Unsigned. *New Republic*, LXX (April 27, 1932), 308.

Unsigned. *Saturday Review of Literature*, VIII (February 13, 1932), 527.

Unsigned. *Spectator*, CXLVII (December 26, 1931), 892.

Unsigned. *Times Literary Supplement* [London], December 3, 1931, p. 978.

Stanboul Train. London: Heinemann, 1932. Also Garden City, New York: Doubleday, Doran, 1932, under the title *Orient Express*.

REVIEWS:

Armstrong, Anne. *Saturday Review*, CLIV (December 24, 1932), 673.

Conrad, George. *Books*, March 12, 1933, p. 10.

Redman, B. R. *Saturday Review of Literature*, IX (March 18, 1933), 489.

Strong, L. A. G. *Spectator*, CXLIX (December 9, 1932), 842.

Unsigned. *Boston Transcript*, March 18, 1933, p. 2.

Unsigned. *The Times* [*London*], December 16, 1932, p. 8e.

Unsigned. *New Republic*, LXXIV (March 22, 1933), 168.

Unsigned. *New York Times*, March 12, 1933, p. 21.

Unsigned. *Pratt*, Summer, 1933, p. 36.

Unsigned. *Time Literary Supplement* [London], December 15, 1932, p. 960.

It's a Battlefield. London: Heinemann, 1934.

REVIEWS:

Bettinger, Beatrice E. *New Republic*, LXXX (September 12, 1934), 139–140.

Paterson, Isabel. *Books*, April 1, 1934, p. 7.

Pritchett, V. S. *Christian Science Monitor*, March 21, 1934, p. 11.

———. *Spectator*, CLVI (February 9, 1934), 206.

Unsigned. *The Times* [*London*], February 6, 1934, p. 19a.

Unsigned. *New York Times*, April 8, 1934, p. 7.

Unsigned. *Times Literary Supplement* [London], February 8, 1934, p. 90.

England Made Me. London: Heinemann, 1935. Also New York: Viking, 1953, under the title *The Shipwrecked*.

REVIEWS:

Benét, W. R. *Saturday Review of Literature*, XII (September 7, 1935), 7.

Carter, Cora. *Books*, September 22, 1935, p. 15.

Hutchison, Percy. *The New York Times Book Review*, Section VI, September 8, 1935, p. 6.

Plomer, William. *Spectator*, CLIV (June 28, 1935), 1116.

Quennell, Peter. *New Statesman and Nation*, IX (June 29, 1935), 964.

Unsigned. *The Times* [London], June 25, 1935, p. 9d.

Unsigned. *Saturday Review*, CLIX (July 27, 1935), 952.

Unsigned. *Times Literary Supplement* [London], July 4, 1935, p. 430.

A Gun for Sale. London: Heinemann, 1936. Also Garden City: Doubleday, Doran, 1936, under the title *This Gun for Hire*.

REVIEWS:

Cuppy, Will. *Books*, June 21, 1936, p. 14.

Ferguson, Otis. *New Republic*, LXXXVII (July 29, 1936), 362.

Hearn, L. Cabot. *Saturday Review of Literature*, XIV (June 27, 1936), 6.

Lehmann, Rosamond. *New Statesman and Nation*, XII (August 1, 1936), 164.

Marsh, F. T. *New York Times*, June 21, 1936, p. 17.

Morton, C. W., Jr. *Boston Transcript*, June 27, 1936, p. 2.

Plomer, William. *Spectator*, CLVII (July 17, 1936), 110.

Unsigned. *New York Times*, July 30, 1952, p. 21.
Unsigned. *Times Literary Supplement* [London], July 11, 1936, p. 579.

Brighton Rock. London: Heineman, 1938.

REVIEWS:

Davenport, Basil. *Saturday Review of Literature*, XVIII (June 25, 1938), 6–7.
Kronenberger, Louis. *New Yorker*, XIV (June 25, 1938), 64.
Marriott, Charles. *Manchester Guardian*, July 26, 1938, p. 7.
Plomer, William. *Spectator*, CLXI (July 15, 1938), 116.
Shawe-Taylor, Desmond. *New Statesman and Nation*, XVI (July 23, 1938), 158.
Southron, J. S. *New York Times*, June 26, 1938, p. 6.
Unsigned. *The Times [London]*, August 26, 1938, p. 15e.
Unsigned. *New Republic*, XCV (July 6, 1938), 260.
Unsigned. *Time*, XXXI (June 27, 1938), 49.
Unsigned. *Times Literary Supplement* [London], July 16, 1938, p. 477.

The Confidential Agent. London: Heinemann, 1939.

REVIEWS:

B[enét], W[illiam] R[ose]. *Saturday Review of Literature*, XX (October 21, 1939), 19–20.
Burnham, Philip. *Commonweal*, XXXI (December 15, 1939), 191.
Gibson, Wilfrid. *Manchester Guardian*, October 6, 1939, 3.
Mair, John. *New Statesman and Nation*, XVIII (September 23, 1939), 432.

Verschoyle, Derek. *Spectator*, CLXIII (September 22, 1939), 418.

Woods, Katherine. *New York Times*, October 1, 1939, p. 20.

Unsigned. *The Times [London]*, September 22, 1939, p. 3d.

Unsigned. *New York Times*, July 30, 1952, p. 21.

Unsigned. *New Yorker*, XV (September 30, 1939), 72.

Unsigned. *Times Literary Supplement* [London], September 23, 1939, p. 553.

The Power and the Glory. London: Heinemann, 1940. Also New York: Viking, 1940, under the title *The Labyrinthine Ways*.

REVIEWS:

Arrowsmith, Jean. *Boston Transcript*, April 20, 1940, p. 2.

Bates, Ralph. *New Republic*, CII (April 22, 1940), 549.

Benét, William Rose. *Saturday Review of Literature*, XXI (March 30, 1940), 5.

Marriott, Charles. *Manchester Guardian*, March 5, 1940, 3.

Marsh, F. T. *New York Times* March 17, 1940, p. 6.

O'Brien, Kate. *Spectator*, CLXIV (March 15, 1940), 390.

Redman, B. R. *Books*, March 31, 1940, p. 3.

Skillin, Edward, Jr. *Commonweal*, XXXI (March 22, 1940), 478.

West, Anthony. *New Statesman and Nation*, XIX (March 16, 1940), 371.

Unsigned. *Atlantic*, CLXV (April 1940), 601.

Unsigned. *Catholic World*, CLI (May 1940), 253.

Unsigned. *The Times [London]*, March 8, 1940, p. 4f.

Unsigned. *New Yorker*, XVI (March 16, 1940), 106.

Unsigned. *Time*, XXXV (April 8, 1940), 88.

Unsigned. *Times Literary Supplement* [London], March 9, 1940, p. 121.

The Ministry of Fear. London: Heinemann, 1943.

REVIEWS:

Chapel, America. *Book Week*, June 6, 1943, p. 4.

Cowley, Malcolm. *New Republic*, CVIII (May 24, 1943), 706.

Estes, Rice. *Library Journal*, LXVIII (May 1, 1943), 363.

Fadiman, Clifton. *New Yorker*, XIX (May 22, 1943), 72.

Gibson, Wilfrid. *Manchester Guardian*, May 21, 1943, 3.

O'Brien, Kate. *Spectator*, CLXX (May 28, 1943), 508.

Rothman, N. L. *Saturday Review of Literature*, XXVI (June 26, 1943), p. 11.

Soskin, William. *Weekly Book Review*, May 30, 1943, p. 4.

Toynbee, Philip. *New Statesman and Nation*, XXV (June 26, 1943), 422.

Wright, Cuthbert. *Commonweal*, XXXVIII (June 4, 1943), 175.

Zabel, M. D. *Nation*, CLVII (July 3, 1943), 18.

Unsigned. *Atlantic*, CLXXII (July 1943), 127.

Unsigned. *Booklist*, XXXIX (July 15, 1943), 464.

Unsigned. *Catholic World*, CLVII (July 1943), 448.

Unsigned. *New York Times*, May 23, 1943, p. 3.

Unsigned. *New York Times*, May 24, 1943, p. 13.

Unsigned. *New York Times*, July 30, 1952, p. 21.

Unsigned. *Time*, XLI (June 14, 1943), 104.

Unsigned. *Times Literary Supplement* [London], May 29, 1943, p. 257.

The Heart of the Matter. London: Heinemann, 1948.

REVIEWS:

Brighouse, Harold. *Manchester Guardian*, May 28, 1948, 3.

Cartmell, Joseph. *Commonweal*, XLVIII (July 16, 1948), 325.

DuBois, William. *New York Times*, July 11, 1948, p. 5.

Hormel, O. D. *Christian Science Monitor*, September 2, 1948, p. 9.

Jackson, J. H. *San Francisco Chronicle*, July 18, 1948, p. 18.

Jones, Ernest. *Nation*, CLXVII (August 21, 1948), 212.

Kennedy, J .S. *Catholic World*, CLXVII (December 1948), 211.

Lewis, E. L. *Library Journal*, LXXIII (April 15, 1948), 651.

McSorley, Joseph. *Catholic World*, CLXVII (September 1948), 564.

Mayberry, George. *New Republic*, CXIX (July 12, 1948), 21.

Orwell, George. *New Yorker*, XXIV (July 17, 1948), 66, 69, 70–71.

Prescott, Orville. *Yale Review*, XXXVIII (Autumn 1948), 191.

Robinson, H. M. *Saturday Review of Literature*, XXXI (July 10, 1948), 3.

Smith, R. D. *Spectator*, CLXXX (June 4, 1948), 686.

Sugrue, Thomas. *New York Herald Tribune Weekly Book Review*, July 11, 1948, p. 1.

Waugh, Evelyn. *Commonweal*, XLVIII (July 16, 1948), 322–325.

Unsigned. *Booklist*, XLIV (July 15, 1948), 382.

Unsigned. *Virginia Kirkus Bookshop Service*, XVI (February 15, 1948), 90.

Unsigned. *Newsweek*, XXXII (July 12, 1948), 84–86.
Unsigned. *Time*, LII (August 9, 1948), 83.
Unsigned. *Times Literary Supplement* [London], May 29, 1948, p. 302.

The Third Man. New York: Viking, 1950.

REVIEWS:

Unsigned. *Times Literary Supplement* [London], August 4, 1950, p. 481.

The End of the Affair. London: Heinemann, 1951.

REVIEWS:

Arnold, G. L. *Twentieth Century*, CLIV (October 1951), 337–342.
Bogan, Louise. *New Republic*, CXXV (December 10, 1951), 29–30.
Downing, Francis. *Commonweal*, LV (December 28, 1951), 298.
Fremantle, Anne. *Saturday Review*, XXXIV (October 27, 1951), 11–12.
Hughes, Riley. *Catholic World*, CLXXIV (January 1952), 312.
Mayberry, George. *New York Times*, October 28, 1951, p. 5.
McLaughlin, Richard. *Theatre Arts*, XXXV (December 1951), 34.
Rolo, C. J. *Atlantic*, CLXXXVIII (November 1951), 88.
Scott, J. D. *New Statesman and Nation*, XLII (September 8, 1951), 258.
Shrapnel, Norman, *Manchester Guardian*, September 7, 1951, 4.
Strong, L. A. G. *Spectator*, CLXXXVII (September 7, 1951), 310.

Sugrue, Thomas. *New York Herald Tribune Book Review*, October 28, 1951, p. 8.

Waugh, Evelyn. *Commonweal*, LIV (August 17, 1951), 458.

———. *The Month*, VI (September 1951), 174–176.

West, Anthony. *New Yorker*, XXVII (November 10, 1951), 154.

Unsigned. *The Times* [*London*], February 25, 1955, p. 11d.

Unsigned. *Times Literary Supplement* [London], September 7, 1951, p. 561.

Loser Takes All. London: Heinemann, 1955.

REVIEWS:

Winterich, John T. *Saturday Review*, XL (October 5, 1957), 17–18.

Unsigned. *Times Literary Supplement* [London], February 18, 1955, p. 101.

The Quiet American. London: Heinemann, 1955.

REVIEWS:

Allen, Walter. *Nation*, CLXXXII (April 21, 1956), 344.

Barr, Donald. *Saturday Review*, XXXIX (March 10, 1956), 12.

Champness, H. M. *Spectator*, CXCV (December 9, 1955), 820.

Clancy, William. *Commonweal*, LXIII (March 16, 1956), 622.

Davis, R. G. *New York Times*, March 11, 1956, pp. 1, 32.

Ghent, Dorothy Van. *Yale Review*, XLV (Summer 1956), 629.

Hackett, Francis. *New Republic*, CXXXV (April 30, 1956), 27.

Hogan, William. *San Francisco Chronicle*, March 9, 1956, p. 17.

Hughes, Riley. *Catholic World*, CLXXXIII (April 1956), 68.

Lehmann, John. *New Republic*, CXXXIV (March 12, 1956), 26.

Liebling, A. J. *New Yorker*, XXXII (April 7, 1956), 148.

O'Donnell, Donat. *New Statesman and Nation*, L (December 10, 1955), 804.

Rolo, C. J. *Atlantic*, CXCVII (March 1956), 82.

Scott, N. A. *Christian Century*, LXXIII (August 1, 1956), 901,

Shrapnel, Norman. *Manchester Guardian*, December 6, 1955, 4.

Stead, Ronald. *Christian Science Monitor*, March 22, 1956, p. 11.

Sullivan, Richard. *Chicago Sunday Tribune*, March 11, 1956, p. 1.

Ullman, J. R. *New York Herald Tribune Book Review*, March 11, 1956, p. 3.

Unsigned. *Booklist*, LII (March 15, 1956), 292.

Unsigned. *Bookmark*, XV (May 1956), 190.

Unsigned. *Time*, LXVII (March 12, 1956), 120.

Unsigned. *Times Literary Supplement* [London], December 9, 1955, p. 737.

Our Man In Havana. London: Heinemann, 1958.

REVIEWS:

Allen, Walter. *New Statesman*, LVI (October 11, 1958), 499.

Cain, J. M. *New York Times*, October 26, 1958, p. 5.

Finn, James. *Commonweal*, LXIX (December 5, 1958), 267.

Hughes, Riley. *Catholic World*, CLXXXVIII (December 1958), 248.

Kermode, Frank. *Spectator*, CCI (October 10, 1958), 496.

Kilpatrick, C. E. *Library Jounral*, LXXXIII (November 15, 1958), 3256.

Maddocks, Melvin. *Christian Science Monitor*, December 4, 1958, p. 17.

Offord, L. G. *San Francisco Chronicle*, December 14, 1958, p. 30.

Rolo, Charles. *Atlantic*, CCII (November 1958), 175.

Sandoe, James. *New York Herald Tribune Book Review*, October 26, 1958, p. 17.

Shebs, R. L. *Chicago Sunday Tribune*, October 26, 1958, p. 8.

Yaffe, James. *Saturday Review*, XLI (November 15, 1958), 19.

Unsigned. *Booklist*, LV (November 1, 1958), 126.

Unsigned. *Virginia Kirkus Bookshop Service*, XXVI (September 1, 1958), 674.

Unsigned. *New Yorker*, XXXIV (November 8, 1958), 209.

Unsigned. *Spectator*, CCI (November 14, 1958), 650.

Unsigned. *Time*, LXXII (October 27, 1958), 94.

Unsigned. *Times Literary Supplement* [London], October 10, 1958, p. 573.

A Burnt-Out Case. London: Heinemann, 1961.

REVIEWS:

Davis, R. G. *New York Times Book Review*, February 19, 1961, p. 4.

Gregor, Ian. *Manchester Guardian*, January 20, 1961, 7.

Hicks, Granville. *Saturday Review*, XLIV (February 18, 1961), 16.

Hughes, Riley. *Catholic World*, CXCIII (April 1961), 47.

Klausler, A. P. *Christian Century*, LXXVIII (May 24, 1961), 653 .

Maddocks, Melvin. *Christian Science Monitor*, February 23, 1961, p. 7.

Mayhew, A. E. *Commonweal*, LXXIV (March 31, 1961), 19.

O'Donnell, Donat. *Spectator*, CCVI (January 20, 1961), 80.

O'Donovan, Patrick. *New Republic*, CXLIV (February 20, 1961), 21.

Pritchett, V. S. *New Statesman*, LXI (January 20, 1961), 102.

Rolo, Charles. *Atlantic*, CCVII (March 1961), 108, 110.

Spector, R. D. *New York Herald Tribune Lively Arts*, February 19, 1961, p. 33.

Sullivan, Richard. *Chicago Sunday Tribune*, February 19, 1961, p. 3.

Warnke, F. J. *Yale Review*, L (June 1961) 631.

Unsigned. *New Yorker*, XXXVII (March 11, 1961), 169.

Unsigned. *Times Literary Supplement* [London], January 20, 1961, p. 37.

A Sense of Reality. London: Bodley Head, 1963.

REVIEWS:

Alter, Robert. *New York Herald Tribune Books*, June 23, 1963, p. 5.

Barrett, William. *Atlantic*, CCXII (July 1963), 128.

Bemis, R. *National Review*, XV (September 24, 1963) 249.

Corke, Hilary. *New Republic*, CXLIX (August 31, 1963), 31.

Furbank, P. N. *Encounter*, XXI (October 1963), 82.

Grumbach, Doris. *Critic*, XXII (August 1963), 84.

Hicks, Granville. *Saturday Review*, XLVI (June 22, 1963), 35.

Hindus, Milton. *The New York Times Book Review*, Section VII, July 14, 1963, p. 4.

MacInnes, C. *Spectator*, CCX (June 21, 1963), 812.

Mayne, Richard. *New Statesman*, LXVI (August 2, 1963), 144.

Prescott, Orville. *The New York Times*, CXII (June 21, 1963), 27.

Quinn, J. J. *Best Sellers*, XXIII (July 15, 1963), 141.

Wilkie, Brian. *Commonweal*, LXXVIII (July 12, 1963), 432.

Unsigned. *New Yorker*, XXXIX (August 19, 1963), 89.

Unsigned. *Time*, LXXXI (June 28, 1963), 87.

Unsigned. *Times Literary Supplement* [London], June 21, 1963, p. 457.

Unsigned. *Virginia Quarterly*, XXXIX (Autumn 1963) 121.

The Comedians. London: Bodley Head, 1966.

REVIEWS:

Bedford, Sybille. *New York Review of Books*, VI (March 3, 1966), 25.

Bowen, John. *New York Times Book Review*, January 23, 1966, p. 1.

Casey, Florence. *Christian Science Monitor*, February 3, 1966, p. 7.

Cheuse, Alan. *Nation*, CCII (February 21, 1966), 218.

Davenport, Guy. *National Review*, XVIII (March 22, 1966), 278.

Gilman, Richard. *New Republic*, CLIV (January 29, 1966), 25.

Griffin, L. W. *Library Journal*, XCI (January 15, 1966), 276.

Jackson, K. G. *Harper's*, CCXXXII (February 1966), 118.

Lodge, David. *Commonweal*, LXXXIII (February 25, 1966), 604.

Murray, J. G. *America*, CXIV (February 5, 1966), 203.

Pritchett, V. S. *New Statesman*, LXXI (January 28, 1966), 129.

Weeks, Edward. *Atlantic*, CCXVII (March 1966), 157.

Unsigned. *Times Literary Supplement* [London], January 27, 1966, p. 57.

THE SERIF SERIES: BIBLIOGRAPHIES AND CHECKLISTS

GENERAL EDITOR: William White, Wayne State University

---

1 *Wilfred Owen (1893-1918): A Bibliography* by William White, with a prefacing note by Harold Owen
SBN: 87338-017-7/ 41pp/ introduction/ preface

2 *Raymond Chandler: A Checklist* by Matthew J. Bruccoli
SBN: 87338-015-0/ ix, 35pp/ introduction

3 *Emily Dickinson, A Bibliography: 1850-1966* by Sheila T. Clendenning
SBN: 87338-016-9/ xxx, 145pp/ preface/ introduction

4 *John Updike: A Bibliography* by C. Clarke Taylor
SBN: 87338-018-5/ vii, 82pp/ introduction

5 *Walt Whitman: A Supplementary Bibliography (1961-1967)* by James T. F. Tanner
SBN 87338-019-3/ vi, 59pp/ introduction

6 *Erle Stanley Gardner: A Checklist* by E. H. Mundell
SBN 87338-034-7/ ix, 91pp/ introduction/ indices

7 *Bernard Malamud: An Annotated Checklist* by Rita Nathalie Kosofsky
SBN 87338-037-1/ xii, 63pp/ preface/ author's note

8 *Samuel Beckett: A Checklist* by J. T. F. Tanner and J. Don Vann
SBN 87338-051-1/ vi, 85pp/ introduction

9 *Robert G. Ingersoll: A Checklist* by Gordon Stein
SBN 87338-047-9/ xxx, 128pp/ preface/ introduction/ index

10 *Jean-Paul Sartre in English: A Bibliographical Guide* by Allen J. Belkind
SBN: 87338-049-5/ xx, 234pp/ preface/ introduction/ index

11 *Tolkien Criticism: An Annotated Checklist* by Richard C. West
SBN: 87338-052-5/ xvi, 73pp/ foreword/ title index

12 *Thomas Wolfe: A Checklist* by Elmer D. Johnson
SBN 87338-050-9/ xiv, 278pp/ introduction

13 *A List of the Original Appearances of Dashiell Hammett's Magazine Work* by E. H. Mundell
SBN 87338-033-9/ viii, 52pp/ preface

14 *Graham Greene: A Checklist of Criticism* by J. Don Vann
SBN 87338-101-7/ vii, 69 pp/ preface

REFERENCE
FOR
USE IN LIBRARY ONLY